What Women In Leadership Need to Stop Doing

Book 4 in the "Stop So You Can Get the Results You Want" Series

BY

LIZ WEBER, CMC, CSP

Also by Liz Weber, CMC, CSP

Something Needs to Change Around Here: The Five Stages to Leveraging Your Leadership

Don't Let 'Em Treat You Like a Girl: A Woman's Guide to Leadership Success

What Business Owners Need to Stop Doing

What Managers Need to Stop Doing

What Human Resources Professionals Need to Stop Doing

Stop So You Can Get The Results You Want

Special Offer

If you enjoyed Liz's insights in this book, take advantage of these special offers:

1. Take Liz's Free Leadership Assessment to determine which of The Five Stages of Focused Leadership® you are currently modeling! Just go to her website, wbsllc.com, to access the assessment!

2. Click here to download Liz's white paper featuring the three things you need to stop today! Go to www.wbsllc.com/stop-it/

Social Media

Visit my website: https://www.WBSLLC.com

Or connect with me on social media:

What Women In Leadership Need to Stop Doing

Book 4 in the "Stop So You Can Get the Results You Want" Series

by Liz Weber

Published 2019 by Aspen Hill Press

This book is licensed for your personal enjoyment and education only. While best efforts have been used, the author and publisher are not offering legal, accounting, medical, or any other professional services advice and make no representations or warranties of any kind and assume no liabilities of any kind with respect to the accuracy or completeness of the contents and specifically disclaim any implied warranties of merchantability or fitness of use for a particular purpose, nor shall they be held liable or responsible to any person or entity with respect to any loss or incidental or consequential damages caused, or alleged to have been caused, directly or indirectly, by the information or programs contained herein. Stories, characters, and entities are 'sanitized' versions of real client experiences.

The information in this book on personnel management is done in an informational manner only. All personnel actions should be reviewed carefully before implementation. Please consult with your human resources professionals, legal counsel etc before taking official action to ensure you are complying with company policies, as well as any and all state and federal employment laws.

All rights reserved. No part of this publication may be reproduced or transmitted in any form or by any means, electronic or mechanical, including photocopying, recording, or by any information storage and retrieval system, without permission in writing from the publisher. All images are free to use or share, even commercially, according to Google at the time of publication unless otherwise noted. Thank you for respecting the hard work of the author(s) and everyone else involved.

Copyright © 2019 by Liz Weber, Weber Business Services, LLC. All Rights Reserved.

Authors and sources cited throughout retain the copyright to their respective materials.

For the loyal fans of my earlier book to women in leadership roles: Don't Let 'Em Treat You Like A Girl: A Woman's Guide to Leadership Success, thank you. Your support of that book inspired me to bridge and expand upon many of the ideas I shared in that book into this one. Your interest in pursuing knowledge, professional challenges, and opportunities to learn, continue to inspire me and educate me. Thank you for being you.

Liz

"With kids, they don't do what you want them to do when you want them to do it. Organizations don't necessarily, either. You've got to listen. You've got to learn how to influence."

Ellen J. Kullman, CEO of E. I. du Pont de Nemours and Company in Wilmington and a former director of General Motors

Contents

Introduction _____ *1*

{ 1 } Stop Focusing On Your OWN Gender _____ *9*

{ 2 } Stop Talking About the Difficulty of Being a Working Mom _____ *19*

{ 3 } Stop Comparing Yourself to Others to Define Your Level of Success _____ *31*

{ 4 } Stop Thinking You Need to Be Perfect to Be a Successful Leader _____ *43*

{ 5 } Stop Focusing on the Details to the Detriment of the Big Picture _____ *53*

{ 6 } Stop Being Quick to Take the Blame For a Mistake or to Accept That Your Idea is Wrong _____ *65*

{ 7 } Stop Saying "Yes" to Everyone While Saying "No" to Yourself _____ *73*

{ 8 } Stop Pouting When You Don't Get Your Way *83*

{ 9 } Stop Avoiding Negotiation _____ *91*

{ 10 } Stop Allowing Others to Tell You Who You Are _____ *115*

Conclusion _____ *125*

Continue Your Leadership Journey _____ *127*

About Liz Weber, CMC, CSP _____ *129*

Introduction

"Stop waiting for a producer. Produce yourself."

— *Marianne Williamson, author, lecturer, and spiritual teacher*

WOMEN LEADERS HAVE a reputation, period, and it's not always undeserved. As I shared in **Don't Let 'Em Treat You Like a Girl - A Woman's Guide to Leadership Success**, it starts in youth: girls, particularly teenage girls, do a lot of dumb things (boys do, too, but we're talking about girls here). Many girls are incredibly insecure, believe their worth and value is determined by their looks, readily belittle themselves, need to talk to one another frequently for validation, and doubt themselves constantly. Hey, I know. I lived it. I grew up with five sisters, and I've raised two daughters. Thankfully, most of us grow out of it.

As adults, however, many women often default to some of the same self-defeating behaviors. Even powerful women in prominent leadership roles occasionally slip into old habits that reinforce old stereotypes. When that happens, women emit signals to everyone around them that they are insecure girls rather than strong, confident women. Honestly, no one likes following someone who comes across as insecure.

If you want to be viewed as a professional—as a leader—you need to be aware of the signals you're sending.

In addition, with the best of intentions, many women in leadership roles, further segregate themselves and other women by claiming women are better managers than men or they choose to support only other women. Because of these self-serving and self-defeating behaviors, women at times sabotage their own professional and leadership success. When you are in a leadership role, people look to you for answers. When they see you segregate yourself, second-guess yourself, whine about being a working mom, take the blame for something that's not your fault, or pout when you don't get your way, they question your leadership abilities.

I'm in no way suggesting that you should deny your womanhood and not look or act like a woman in the workplace. I'm in no way suggesting you should not support other women. I'm suggesting that when you focus on being a woman and take your "femaleness" a bit too far and you make it your defining characteristic, you become one of those "women leaders" that people lump into stereotypes. You're described as a woman leader who's a witch or a woman leader who is something else. You're not simply described as a leader. Don't allow the fact that you're a woman take precedence over being a manager, a CEO, or a committee chair. It's no different than focusing more on being Jewish than being a senior programmer.

As a leader, there are professional skills and traits that are expected. It's your job to identify and exhibit them so you can be challenged and judged professionally as a leader—and not as a woman.

Your responsibility, regardless of your position, is to do that job. The fact that you're Jewish or a woman is just that—a fact. Be proud of it. Be proud of being African-American or whatever your race. Be proud of your age. Be proud of who you are. But then remember, in any situation in which you are expected to provide guidance and leadership, your responsibility as a leader is to be a leader. The people who put you in that position and the people who support you in that position expect you to do the job, fulfill its responsibilities, and to fulfill the role. So, be smart. Be intentional. Choose, and then become, the type of leader you want to be.

"It is our choices that show what we truly are far more than our abilities."

— *J.K. Rowling, author*

{ 1 } Stop Focusing On Your OWN Gender

"The more women help one another, the more we help ourselves. Acting like a coalition truly does produce results. Any coalition of support must also include men, many of whom care about gender inequality as much as women do."

— *Sheryl Sandberg, COO, Facebook*

WHY: BY FOCUSING on supporting your own gender and putting your mentoring and leadership development efforts primarily behind only women, you're perpetuating the exact behavior you're trying to correct (i.e. reverse discrimination!). Also, by focusing frequently on supporting only other women, you're focusing your colleagues, employees, team members, and others on it too. You and they need to focus on talents, not gender—yours and everyone else's.

Our world is a world in which men and women work together—a mixed workplace. It's diversity of the first order. Men and women innately think differently, but when we work in the same business culture, we all have to abide by the cultural norms of the organization, rather than by norms defined by gender or stereotypes.

This means that men have to cut the macho crap, but women need to cut the "girly" stuff too.

For example, when some women reach their vision of success, they stop, pivot and then focus on helping only other women advance. Following the success of her bestselling book, *Lean In: Women, Work, and the Will to Lead*, author Sheryl Sandberg established Lean In, a foundation focused on helping women. It's great that Sheryl's helping women. Her foundation provides a community that fosters motivation, and it provides women some wonderful tools to develop leadership skills and support their drive for success. However, might it not have an even bigger impact if she used her position, professional network, experience, skills, and leadership insights to help both women AND men? Why not demonstrate to women AND men how to manage both sexes, how to work smarter together, and how to be effective leaders so both genders succeed? Why separate and segregate?

Use your position, professional network, experience, skills, and leadership insights to help both women AND men.

In the workplace, a manager's role is to leverage the talents of the people for whom he or she is responsible. It's not the manager's role to support only the female employees or only the male employees. It's the manager's role to support all the employees she or he is responsible to lead.

That's what the focus needs to be—not creating a "preferred" class, or what is often unintentionally conveyed: additional support is provided the needy class of women in up-and-coming or current leadership roles who obviously have more issues than the men do. Every person has issues. Every person needs help. Every person in the workforce needs support at various times to learn, move forward, and become a better person and professional.

However, when women in leadership only focus on supporting other women, they exclude the many gifted and deserving men on their teams and in the workplace who also have much to offer.

For years, my company has provided women in leadership training programs for various organizations to support their efforts in strengthening their female managers' leadership skills as well as to provide stronger networking opportunities for the women. They've been terrific. The programs have been helpful to the participants as they've shared solid leadership concepts and have enabled many of them to develop strong professional networks.

However, the programs have been most helpful to the organizations' leadership teams as the programs have helped *them* focus on supporting their leaders as individuals and leadership teams—not by classifying them by gender. As a result, several of my clients have started to phase out of the women-only programs, and are now simply expanding these leadership development programs to focus on team-wide leadership development, increased team awareness, emotional intelligence, cross-personality and gender communications—for *all* leaders regardless of gender. The roughly five percent of the program that was specifically targeted to women has remained with only slight modification to highlight special general traits in women and special characteristics of men—both sexes laugh; both sexes learn.

As a result, these organizations are more comfortably moving away from focusing on women in leadership roles to focusing on creating more functional cross-gender, cross-cultural, cross-generational teams. Likewise, the segregated training participants are more comfortably moving away from viewing themselves as different and having issues men couldn't possibly understand, to realizing every manager and every employee has challenges. How one deals with them is what matters.

Here's what I suggest you do instead: Support whichever causes you believe are right and necessary. If you choose to support primarily women—fine. However, as a leader, model what a true leader does: provide intentional, customized, and focused coaching, mentoring and support to others depending on their true needs—not simply because of their gender—because not all women have the same leadership development or support needs.

Do not hide or not discuss gender when it is appropriate. Being a woman is a great thing. However, so is being a man. Don't use gender as a crutch or excuse or the sole reason you support another in the workplace. Focus on people not genders. That's what effective leaders do.

"I actually have never been gender-conscious in business. I find that it detracts from your drive and your passion."

— *Martha Stewart, founder and chairman of Martha Stewart Living Omnimedia*

{ 2 } Stop Talking About the Difficulty of Being a Working Mom

"So tell me again how hard it is working full time and being a mother. No other mother that works here has ever had that problem."

— *Greeting Card Insert*

WHY: MANY OF us are or have been working parents too. We don't have a lot of sympathy for you. We know the tough decisions we had to make, and how we had to struggle to juggle our work and parenting responsibilities every 24 hours. Now it's your turn because you've made your own choices.

On March 5, 2014, the online news magazine, *Slate*, published an article about work-life balance and how men and women see the issue differently. The article cited a study conducted by the Harvard Business School, in which 4,000 male and female executives were interviewed about conflicts they experience between their work and home lives.

Not surprisingly, more of the men chose work without guilt, knowing their best contribution to their families was as "breadwinners," while the women expressed more ambivalence. They expressed pride as a result of their career successes but also had trouble reconciling their roles at home. Would their kids still turn out all right if they were raised by nannies? Had they made the wrong decision by being so ambitious at work? Even the women who had chosen not to have children for fear that their careers would suffer seemed tentative about that choice. The point is, all of it is just that; a choice.

Make a choice on what your balanced work-life will be: will you focus more of your time and energies at work or more time with family? It's your right to choose. You will have to choose and you may have to make that choice every day. But whatever you choose, realize no one's life is in perfect balance. There's always some "give" to allow another something to "take" more of your time and energy. You choose which is which. Your career shouldn't be your focus in life to the exclusion of your family. But neither should your family be the focus of your life to the exclusion of your career if you choose to have one. Make a choice as to how you'll balance your life.

Besides, no one likes whiners. No one likes listening to them or being around them. Most people ignore them, walk away from them, and lose respect for them. I'm sorry if this offends you, but most people you work with don't want to hear how chaotic your life is or how hard you work. If your life is chaotic because of your kids' schedules, cut back on the extracurricular activities. Your problem is not unique, and there are ways to resolve it. But you have to make your choice and then live with it. Your choice certainly doesn't need to be debated with your co-workers. They don't care.

Most people you work with don't want to hear how hard your life is or how hard you work. They care how well you do your job.

Several years ago I was conducting a training program for a group of up-and-coming women leaders. During our working lunch, I conducted a table talk and asked each woman to share a tip or idea she had that enabled her to be more productive. Several women shared logical insights into how they multi-tasked or incorporated technology into their lives to serve as their virtual assistants.

When it was 'Susan's' turn, she smiled smugly. Susan had been late every morning for the three-day program. However, she now said, "My husband and I take our family out to eat every night. That way, I don't have to worry about cooking and cleaning. With three small children, you can't imagine how hard it is to get everything done: get them from school and daycare, make dinner, clean up the dishes, and then get the kids ready for bed. By eating out every night, I don't have that stress as a working mom anymore."

To say the other women were stunned, as was I, is an understatement. Before most of us could respond, one woman blurted out, "You go out to eat every night just because you have three kids? I've got four kids under the age of six and there's no way my husband and I could afford to do that nor would we want to!"

Needless to say, other women had comments they wanted to express, but I turned the conversation into sharing tips with Susan has to how she could refocus her view of her role, her husband's and that of her children in balancing their lives. In her attempt to succeed over her Wonder Woman view of what she thought she needed to do as a working mother (i.e., take care of all the morning child-care duties and transportation, work a full day and also do all the cooking, cleaning, and child care chores too), Susan had simply shifted those responsibilities to various restaurants, instead of sharing them at home with her husband and children.

When I suggested to Susan she have her children help with setting the table and cleaning up the dishes at a bare minimum, she replied,

"They're only 5, 4, and 3 years old." To which I replied, "So?" She stared at me stunned. I continued:

"Susan at 5, 4, and 3, I anticipate your children know what a plate, fork, knife, and spoon are. If they're old enough to know what basic dinner utensils are and how to use them to feed themselves, they're old enough to help put them on the table, and also put them in the dishwasher when dinner is done. By making them help you each night, you'll also be teaching them how to take care of themselves. Having your children help with chores helps them learn self-reliance too."

The other women shared insights into how they had created a divide and conquer process with their husbands to more equitably divide the household and parenting chores. None of the insights were earth-shatteringly unique. They were simply outlined to address tasks typical families need to take care of and then divvied up (age-appropriately) among the capable persons in the family. No working mom needs to bear all the burden. But whatever burden she chooses—she chooses.

Here's what I suggest you do instead: Model for your kids how to be a parent who makes the best decisions she can in balancing her roles as a mom and as a professional.

Sometimes your job needs to take a backseat; sometimes your kids will have to wait their turn for your time. It won't hurt your kids to learn they can't be the center of your attention all the time. It's your life—choose what your priorities are and to which you will focus your love, passions, attention, and time.

> *"She did it all because she wanted to do it all. There was none of this complaining about how she'd make it work—the husband, the job, the house, the kids."*
>
> *— Candace Bushnell, author, Sex and the City*

{ 3 } Stop Comparing Yourself to Others to Define Your Level of Success

"When I got to the top, my financial rewards were very high, but my psychic income bank account was nearly empty... I wanted to be more creative again."

— *Maxine Clark, founder and CEO, Build-a-Bear Workshop*

WHY: MOST PEOPLE who present themselves as confident and successful just have a different "scale" they are using to gauge their success. More often than not, I've experienced that when I've finally "arrived," and I'm interacting with others who I'd anticipated were much more successful than I, they weren't more successful. They just had a different set of criteria and level of performance than I had been using. They projected success because they'd achieved what they believed made them successful. Also, keep in mind, we often only hear about the successes of others; we don't often hear about the number of failures they endured along the way.

I've seen people who believe they want power, money, and the top spot, when what they really want is the self-confidence and financial contentedness they see in those they view as successful. This may go against what you intellectually believe leadership success is, which is why you struggle with your current level of success. When you're not satisfied with what you have, your lack of self-confidence kicks in.

Here's the truth: you don't need to have a lot of money to be financially content and self-confident. You just have to know what amount of financial wealth will make you content and also identify why you lack self-confidence. Most importantly, you need to identify for yourself - honestly - what will make you feel happy and successful. Whatever it is, it's right for you. It doesn't matter if it isn't right for someone else.

I enjoy studying successful people. I'm constantly watching others to see how they do their thing. I'm often amazed that, when you watch others who are "successful," they make what they do look so easy. Yet it comes from years of practice, experience, learning the hard way, and refinement to become more focused and—yes—confident in who they are and what they do. Identify others you deem "successful leaders." Study them. Watch them. Identify what they do that resonates with others, with their employees, and with their clients. Identify what resonates with you. If something resonates with you, it's more likely to work for you when you apply it. It may just be that you need to get out of your own way and realize you have good momentum going already.

When one of my best friends from college, Diana, and I turned thirty, we kept a promise we'd made to each other to reconnect in person at age thirty. Diana had just been promoted to a senior management position within state government, and I had started my own company. As we shared stories about our careers, we realized we had recently had a similar epiphany: We had both reached a milestone of "success" in our respective careers, but what we thought we'd feel when we achieved it, we didn't. The anticipated feelings of greater professional confidence and financial security were there.

However, we'd both assumed that by now working more closely with senior-level people, we would somehow finally access "success" as we'd be working with brighter and more successful people; people who "had it together."

We often only hear about the successes of others; we don't often hear about the number of failures they endured along the way.

What Diana and I found instead was that we were just working with people who had traveled the same paths we had, only they'd done it before us. Many of the senior managers and executives we were now working with, were no more successful or smarter than we were. In fact, by our scales, they were often less successful given their crazy travel schedules, work pressures, and relationship and family time challenges they struggled to manage.

We also realized, these high-level professionals were only human. Some managers would say or do things that weren't all that brilliant. In fact, they would say or do things that would make Diana or me sit back and think to ourselves, "You're a senior manager and you really believe that? You honestly think THAT's the best approach for handling this situation?"

These epiphanies were so insightful for us, not because they made us feel superior or smarter than they. Not at all. They were important insights for us because until then, both Diana and I had believed we weren't as smart or successful as we were supposed to be because of how we saw others. We were judging ourselves incorrectly and super-imposing an unrealistic scale on others.

We realized they weren't smarter than us. They had simply experienced more than us. They also simply managed their personal and professional lives differently. Sure they made more money than we had been making and therefore they had nicer cars and bigger homes. But again, those were simply because they'd had more time to gather the financial wherewithal to purchase those things. But they still had challenges with their relationships, children, families, health, personal finances, and a myriad of other things. They just didn't trumpet their failures and challenges. They focused on achieving and maintaining the successes that were important to them.

Successful people are human too. They've got strengths, challenges, and successes—and they're theirs. But, we have our own strengths and the right to determine what successes we will pursue.

Here's what I suggest you do instead: Realize you're more successful than you give yourself credit for being. Then spend time formulating a clear vision for what future success looks like for you. What type of life, career, and family arrangement do you want? What type of career or personal life will allow you to leverage what you already enjoy and do well? If you don't know, focus on what others appreciate about what you do, who you are, and how you make them feel. Identify who your "fans" are and clarify what it is that YOU do so well that positively impacts the lives of others. Then go out and do more of it. Remember: You may have already achieved more than you realize.

> *"The reason we struggle with insecurity is because we compare our behind-the-scenes with everyone else's highlight reel."*
>
> *— Steve Furtick, bestselling author and Lead Pastor of Evolution Church in Charlotte, NC*

{ 4 } Stop Thinking You Need to Be Perfect to Be a Successful Leader

"I think it's a useful concept to realize that just because you didn't get exactly what you wanted doesn't mean you didn't get something that's really good."

— *Debora Spar, President, Barnard College*

WHY: MOST OTHER people aren't looking for perfection; they're just looking for the basics to move them forward. Understand what people are really expecting from you and focus on delivering that much.

Most managers and organizational leaders are under incredible amounts of pressure to perform. Yet, much of the pressure is self-imposed. It's a result of being so busy being busy; they're not doing what they're really supposed to do. It's the result of confusing Doing with Managing or Leading. You have to let go of controlling all of the details (Doing) in order to help others do what they need to be doing (Managing) so you can deliver what people truly need from you (Leadership).

Perfectionism is also what holds so many back from interacting comfortably with others or advancing professionally. Quite often, the tasks they're obsessing over trying to make perfect, don't need to be perfect; they just need to get done.

In an executive coaching session with Bill, a Regional Director, he expressed his frustration with one of his managers, Mary. She spent so much time on projects and getting him information, it drove him crazy. She did good work; it just took her too long for his liking— and then she'd get resentful and frustrated when he'd ask for something else. In a subsequent coaching session with Mary, she too expressed her frustrations in working with and communicating with Bill.

Mary could tell Bill was frequently frustrated with the amount of time it took her to give him information. Yet, in order to give him the financial projections he wanted, she needed hours if not days to properly calculate and proof the numbers. Then, within a day, Bill would ask her for a different number or set of numbers. He was never satisfied! It drove her nuts. Nothing she did ever seemed good enough.

Most other people aren't looking for perfection; they're just looking for the basics to move them forward. Understand what people are really expecting from you, and focus on delivering that much.

In talking the situation through with Mary, it became obvious, she was obsessing over trying to provide perfect numbers when Bill didn't want or need perfect numbers. He needed a zone, a range, or some initial target to use in his high-level planning to determine if the direction of potential strategies he and the other directors were considering were on target. Bill needed to know basically if a projected number was roughly 5,000 units or 50,000 units.

Based upon which end of that zone the potential number would be, he and the other directors could then refine their strategies. Once they knew which end of the zone the projected number was pointing them towards, Bill would then ask for another or a different number to again, help him hone in on his target.

Yet, in trying to be absolutely correct and perfect, Mary would spend hours if not days, calculating that the most probable number was 12,937, only to have Bill reply the next day and ask for a number closer to the 50,000 units range. Being perfect wasn't important. Being clear in what information would be needed and how it would be used—was. Once Bill understood he needed to be more clear and Mary understood she needed to ask how Bill wanted to use the numbers he was requesting, she was able to more quickly provide him with the type of information he needed.

Given the often, grey and risky nature of the decisions they have to make, many CEOs and senior managers don't know specifically what they're looking for—they just know they need to see preliminary information, data, trends, or other material to help them piece a strategy together or to confirm a decision. It's one of those, "I won't know until I see it" scenarios.

Given their experience in decision-making and problem solving, they may need to see two, three, four or more iterations of the same information before they can most comfortably make a decision. That's normal. It's still frustrating for the person or team that has to generate all the material for them to review, but it's needed, it's helpful and it's natural. So don't take it personally that your original submission wasn't "right." It simply may not have been right at that time for that reason.

If you're over-complicating things in your quest for perfection, stop.

Here's what I suggest you do instead: Identify what the real issue or subject is and what is being sought from you. Figure out the level of input that is needed from you so that you can provide that level of input or feedback instead of creating more work—and incorrect work—for yourself. Also, realize that you don't constantly have to "over-deliver," because all you're really doing is putting extra pressure on yourself. All the other person expects is "what they asked for" so they can move forward.

To keep things in perspective, ask yourself (maybe even write yourself a note): "Am I making this harder than it needs to be?" and, "Does this matter to anyone other than me?" If you're over-complicating things in your quest for perfection, stop. If the task doesn't matter to anyone other than yourself, is it worth your time and effort—or are your efforts better spent elsewhere?

> *"No one would deny that it's smart to set high standards for yourself... However... It's dumb when to desire to be 100 percent perfect leads to zero accomplishment."*
>
> *— Dr. Arthur Freeman, author and clinical psychologist*

{ 5 } Stop Focusing on the Details to the Detriment of the Big Picture

"The question I ask myself like almost every day is, 'Am I doing the most important thing I could be doing?'"

— *Mark Zuckerberg, founder, Facebook*

WHY: LEADERS FOCUS on where they want to take their organization and how to move it in that direction. They don't care who does the work, they just want it done. Effective leaders quickly and comfortably delegate work down and throughout their teams to keep things moving forward. In contrast, if you don't effectively delegate but instead stay focused on the details and the tactical implications of a decision or action, you solidify others' perception of you as a tactical, front-line team member, or working supervisor.

Supervisors and managers focus on production here and now—in the relative short-term and in getting the work done through their team members. Leaders think: "In addition to everything we currently need to do, what else should I be focusing on to move this organization forward?" Leaders think about the future. They think about moving the organization forward as a whole. Again, they don't focus too much on who is going to do the work; they focus on what needs to get done. Effective leaders are constantly scanning their organization to identify which area they need to focus on next to ensure all departments, facilities, and operations are moving forward together.

If you seek a higher-level leadership position within an organization, realize you need to behave and think at the higher level -- as leaders do. Front-line team members tend to focus on their own areas of responsibility and the technicalities of how the work will get done.

Effective front-line doers develop and utilize systems and processes to help them do their jobs efficiently, but they still do the work themselves.

Supervisors and managers tend to focus on their own areas and how best to effectively leverage their teams' skills and resources to get the work done. Leaders look to the future. Leaders look at the big picture and constantly assess how well the organization is moving forward.

All that is said to suggest you focus on how effective leaders think. If you can identify, what key performance indicators, what metrics are important to them, you will have broken their code and will be able to help them focus on and create the big picture vision they're pursuing. Are they focused on revenues, market share, market influence, product reach, brand recognition, or customer satisfaction? What markers of success do they view as important? If you can help them identify and enhance those, you'll position yourself as a leader instead of a tactical team member with limited capabilities to see the big picture.

If you can help other leaders identify and enhance their key performance indicators, you'll more solidly position yourself as a leader instead of a tactical team member with limited capabilities to see the big picture.

During a client's strategic planning session, Rena, a senior-level IT manager had a near nervous breakdown. Rena was an amazingly, loyal and dedicated employee. She would willingly come in early and stay late to help with production. She would also spend hours working on various spreadsheets and reports herself making sure all the data were correct, logical and organized. Rena had vast amounts of data she would collect, manipulate, and study. She didn't trust her team to manage the data, she controlled the data and the reports so she could ensure their accuracy.

As I was leading the senior team, including Rena, in identifying their key performance indicators (KPI), each manager shared what data he or she was already capturing that would fulfill the newly refined KPIs to help drive the organization forward. When it was Rena's turn to share, she proudly shared just a sampling of the various reports and data she already had.

As she spoke, I watched as few around the table seemed to view her information as exciting. Finally, the CEO spoke, "Rena, who uses those reports?"

"Well, I do and I share information from them with managers and employees when they ask for it," she responded defensively. The CEO continued, "I'm sure your reports are interesting, but how does that information help us generate revenue and increase market share?"

As that question registered with her, I could see by her eyes she was facing a huge internal struggle, as she had no viable answer to his question. Her reports were informative, interesting, and correct—but she had become so focused on them and analyzing them for her own benefit, she hadn't thought of them in a bigger-picture perspective. The data was "hers" and it was correct based upon daily activities.

However, she hadn't thought to look at the information as strategic to analyze the data in a more whole-company perspective to help drive revenues and market share.

After the strategy session, Rena spent several days thinking about her work, her reports, and the data she gathered. Because she'd been challenged on the value of her work, she had to view it differently. It wasn't easy for her to get over the initial feelings of failure and to reevaluate the real value of her work, but she did.

Once she did, it was as if a whole new, exciting world opened up to her. She now understood the bigger-picture value she could provide the leadership team by reformatting and aligning her reports to the leadership team's and the company's KPIs. She'd had the data all along; she just wasn't seeing the big-picture value it contained for the larger organization. Rena now understood how to think and behave less tactically and more strategically. She now understood how to think as a leader and focus on the big picture.

Here's what I suggest you do instead: Clearly understand what metrics, what key performance indicators (KPIs), and what issues are driving the leadership team's strategies and decisions. If you don't know them, find out.

Learn to analyze the metrics and KPIs. Become comfortable with how their changes and shifts affect strategy. You can't and won't be respected as a leadership team peer until you can help the team move their goals forward, and keep score the way they do.

> *"I used to think, 'If I don't do it, it won't get done right.' I have realized that I cannot do everything... delegating is a better approach to getting more done."*
>
> — *Alpa Shah, CEO, 1st American Systems and Services*

{ 6 } Stop Being Quick to Take the Blame For a Mistake or to Accept That Your Idea is Wrong

"I'd get kicked out of buildings all day long, people would rip up my business card in my face... but I knew I could sell and I wanted to sell something I had created."

— *Sara Blakely, founder, Spanx*

WHY: WHEN YOU quickly or willingly accept someone else's opinion that your idea, work, or input is "wrong," you diminish your credibility.

Be willing to back up and stand up for your ideas and work. Understand that often what is most helpful to effective managers is contrarian and differing opinions. Why? They force a more 360-degree review of an issue. By not sharing your ideas, you're depriving the other managers of the opportunity to take a more holistic view of the issue. As a result, you're not helping the team arrive at a truly well-thought-out answer or decision.

As a respected leader, people need to see that you can stand your ground. Many managers and leaders I've worked with want you to defend your position. When you do, it causes them to think harder, deeper, and sometimes more completely. It causes them to mentally if not overtly defend their position as well. Again, this back and forth leads to better, more well-thought-out decisions and strategies.

Rick, a CEO recently shared with me the benefits he reaps when his team members pushback. It challenges him and makes him think harder. Rick was fairly new into his role as CEO when he started asking and challenging his managers to defend their positions or information they were submitting to him to ensure they had vetted each idea to its fullest. One of his senior managers, Anna, was initially irritated and confused as to why he was pushing her to provide more detail. "Why are you challenging me? Don't you trust my judgment and abilities?" she'd ask.

Even though he had talked with her several times privately, Anna felt attacked because she'd not had to defend her research and recommendations to the prior CEO. However, after the debate-filled senior team meetings became the new norm, Anna learned to confidently present and defend her recommendations and positions. She no longer viewed the CEO and the other managers' challenges as personal attacks, but for what they were: professional challenges to ensure all senior team strategies and recommendations were well-thought-out and vetted.

When you effectively defend your position or recommendation, you cause others to think harder and deeper about their own positions and ideas.

Anna realized Rick's actions weren't personal challenges. They were actions to cause Anna - and every other member of his senior team—to think deeper about their work. By doing so, they each would be better positioned to debate on the merits of the various strategies they were to discuss and decide as a senior team. His challenges weren't personal. They were intentional.

Here's what I suggest you do instead: Do your job and provide ideas and work that require your skill, expertise, and analysis. Do it to the best of your ability; then stand behind it. Defend it. If your work ultimately is found lacking or wrong, learn from the experience and move on. Don't run, hide, or retreat. Stay engaged, and incorporate what you've learned the next time.

Knowing when and how to stand your ground, as well as when and how much to clarify your position, is critical. You don't need to debate every point. You also won't make everyone happy with every decision you make. So make them and move on. You need to get things done. Be a leader. Be willing to stand your ground, defend your stance when necessary, and keep moving forward.

> *"Never apologize. Never explain. Just get the thing done and let them howl."*
>
> *— Agnes Macphail, former member of Canadian Parliament*

{ 7 } Stop Saying "Yes" to Everyone While Saying "No" to Yourself

"Take care of yourself first so that you can take care of others."

— *Frances Weber, my mother*

WHY: WHEN YOU overextend yourself, you run the risk of burning out quickly. When you ignore your own physical, mental, emotional, and spiritual needs, you become tired and resentful. When that happens you simply can't be an effective leader. When you're exhausted, how can you motivate and be focused on supporting a team—who you may well resent because of all you already do to support them?

Marissa is a married mother of three very active children, aged 15, 13, and 10. Each child is typically involved with at least one after-school and weekend sport. Marissa's husband is establishing himself in a new job, travels extensively, and is also the coach for several youth soccer teams. Marissa and her family have a loving, close-knit extended family that gathers every Thursday evening and Sunday. She is an incredible mother who truly adores her children and family. Marissa is also a dedicated employee who works full-time.

One of Marissa's joys in life is helping and supporting (physically and emotionally) others. However, she often does it at her own expense. During the past school year, with her husband's new work and travel schedule, Marissa had to bear the brunt of many of the parenting responsibilities herself. In addition to getting her kids to and from school, to and from sports practices and matches (five to six days a week), to and from family gatherings, as well as helping them understand and complete their homework and science projects, her grandmother became ill.

In addition, her job changed dramatically. Without notice, she was promoted, yet it didn't feel that way to her. Many of her key responsibilities were redistributed and outsourced. The way she had worked so contentedly for the prior eight years had been completely disrupted. She used to go to work and immerse herself in projects as a mental escape from her busy family schedule and personal pressures.

However, now she was being forced to think and work differently. Marissa felt like a failure. Her work sanctuary and key projects had been yanked away from her. Her kids were battling colds, homework and science projects, her husband was struggling with his new job, and her family was arguing over how best to care for

Grandma. Marissa gave of herself and focused on supporting them all. Until she got sick.

For the first time in over 15 years, Marissa was so ill she was forced to stay in bed for four days. In the past, when she'd feel ill, she'd still take care of her family and go to work. However, this time, she couldn't get out of bed. She could barely move or talk. She was physically, emotionally, and mentally exhausted. Her husband and her kids were worried, "You're never sick! What's wrong with you?" Her body had reached its limit to function further. It needed rest. Luckily, after four days of sleep and bed-rest, she woke up physically, emotionally, and mentally "better."

During a follow-up visit with her physician, Marissa's physician asked her to share what was happening in her life. After Marissa relayed her life over the past several months, her physician said, "Marissa, I'm going to teach you something." The physician then wrote on a pad of paper and turned the paper for Marissa to view. It said: NO!

"Learn to say and use this word Marissa. Here's another word I'd like you to learn." The physician again wrote on her pad of paper. This time, when she turned the pad to Marissa, it said: HELP. "Saying 'No' to others and asking for help doesn't mean you're a failure. It means you understand your limits. We all have them."

As a result, Marissa made several decisions. She decided her family no longer needed to attend the family gatherings every Thursday evening. That alone would enable her to regain one night of quiet with her husband and children. She stopped volunteering during the sporting events in which her children played. Instead she'd attend to simply watch her children play. She reviewed her new work responsibilities and realized she'd actually have to do less work herself. She also focused on her grandmother and made health care decisions that her grandmother wanted, not what other family members wanted. She stopped trying to support and please everyone. It was all... a relief.

Here's what I suggest you do instead: Just as flight attendants instruct you to put on your own mask before assisting others, be sure to tend to your own needs. Know your own body's stress signals before they become too severe to remedy. Learn what recharges your batteries when you get too overwhelmed. Take a personal day or a vacation if you need to recharge. Outsource a project. Hire additional staff. Bring on a contract employee or two. Delegate a task if you need to, but most importantly, as a person, understand you don't have to do everything others ask of you. Make your professional and personal systems and processes work for you.

If you've been working 80-90 hour workweeks and are feeling as if you don't have a life anymore, how much of that time have you spent developing or delegating to others or identifying ways to eliminate or automate time-consuming tasks? My experience tells me—very little. Take stock of your personal and professional stressors. If you feel overwhelmed, make some changes. Take care of yourself.

"Learn to say 'no' to the good so that you can say 'yes' to the best."

— John C Maxwell, author, The 21 Indispensible Qualities of a Leader: Becoming the Person Others Will Want to Follow

{ 8 } Stop Pouting When You Don't Get Your Way

"Maturity is the ability to think, speak, and act your feelings within the bounds of dignity."

— *Jim Rohn, author and motivational speaker*

WHY: YOU'RE AN adult. When you don't get your way or something doesn't work out correctly, trying to act "cute" by pouting, or worse yet, sticking out your bottom lip and making a "pouty boo-boo" face doesn't make you or the situation "cute." You're not five years old. You simply look silly and immature.

I recently encountered a woman in a fireplace store who popped out a boo-boo lip because her new fireplace insert wasn't big enough. I looked at her and almost said, "Seriously? You've got to be pushing your mid-30s and you're doing the boo-boo lip thing I ended with my daughters when they were five!"

As a leader, this type of childish behavior is simply... embarrassing. You can't pout and behave as a whiny five-year-old when you're expected to lead others. Your team will not respect you. Period.

When you don't get your way or something doesn't turn out as you'd planned, take alternative action. But don't pout! For example: have you ever been in a meeting and you shared an idea, but no one paid any attention to it? Yet ten minutes later when someone else said basically the same thing, everyone jumped at the idea praising him for his brilliance! Then, because you were so frustrated, you sat back in your chair, folded your arms and thought to yourself, "That was my idea! No one ever listens to me around here. I don't even know why they invite me to these meetings. They never pay attention to anything I say anyway. I might as well not even be here."

You pouted. You disconnected. You disengaged. You stopped behaving as a leader. You also stopped behaving as a contributing member of the team sitting around that table. Each of those behaviors is unacceptable. None of them are cute.

Behave as an adult, not a child, or you'll be treated as one.

If an idea you introduced is initially ignored, instead of getting angry, pouting and relinquishing your spot at the table, do your job and maintain your position. When your initial comment falls on deaf ears, tell yourself it wasn't the right idea at the right time. However, when someone else says what you had said earlier, instead of shutting down, speak up. Say something along the lines of, "Fred thank you for bringing this up again! This is what I was trying to share earlier when I said... Let me explain that a bit more..." Retake ownership of your idea.

If your idea is subsequently challenged and you don't have more to immediately add to the discussion, don't shut down. If you don't know what else to add to the conversation immediately, simply look at the other person(s) and ask, "I'm at a loss as to what to do next.

What ideas do you have?" Then look at them and wait for an answer. Stay engaged and committed to finding a solution.

Here's what I suggest you do instead: If something doesn't "work" or doesn't go your way, don't pout and don't shut down. You're going to have a harder time trying to "sell" or to get others to have confidence in you and the strength of your future ideas if you've got a history of pouting when others don't back your views or you don't get your way. Face the fact that life isn't fair.

As a manager, as a leader, you are constantly making choices, recommendations, and decisions. Many of them will be right. Some of them will be wrong. Others will agree with some of your ideas, but not all. That's life and that's part of your job as a leader. Your job is to identify opportunities and actions you believe appropriate for your team and the organization. If others and the powers that be agree and support you—great. If they challenge your idea, do your homework and defend your position. If they still don't agree with you, let it go. You've done your job; they've done theirs.

"Don't find a fault, find a remedy; anybody can complain."

— Henry Ford, founder, Ford Motor Company

{ 9 } Stop Avoiding Negotiation

"Women have systematically lower expectations. The problem with having systematically lower expectations is that you get systematically lower outcomes... So, they get less not because they are women, but because their expectations are lower."

—*Margaret Neale, Negotiations Professor at Stanford's Graduate School of Business*

WHY: THERE HAS been a lot of talk in the media about the "pay gap" between men and women, even when both a man and a woman hold the same type of position such as CEO. All the discussion, frustration, and anger about the pay disparity is valid and justified. In positions where either a man or woman could hold the job, rightly or wrongly, there are still often comments made such as, "Well he has to support his entire family..." and "Well her husband is a high-level executive with...."

What one's spouse does or does not do for work—and therefore to contribute to the household income—is irrelevant. Unless a position has a need for one specific gender to fulfill it versus another, there is no rationale for gender-based comparisons. However, the pay gap exists.

True, there are some careers with more women in them than men, such as teaching, nursing, and retail sales, which have had historically lower pay scales. Regardless, situations involving pay disparity are inexcusable.

However, an idea for which women in leadership roles need to review is the one presented by Linda Babcock, Ph.D.: Women and men negotiate differently for pay raises, promotions, and salaries. The key difference: Many women don't negotiate at all.

As a woman, as a leader, if you cannot confidently and effectively negotiate with others as to why you deserve the salary, fee, or rate you're requesting, why should they give it to you? You need to be able to articulate the value of what you bring to justify the money they will pay you. It's as simple as that—but it's not easy until you understand how to define and "sell" your value.

Negotiate as hard for yourself as you would for someone else.

In the sales world, those who have achieved the greatest success are those who don't focus on selling the features of the widgets or whatever they're selling, but instead focus on selling the benefits their widgets provide. As an example, personal lending officers in banks are more effective in 'selling' home equity loans when they focus on a benefit the home equity loan can offer versus the home equity loan itself.

No one wakes up in the morning and says, "I want a home equity loan!" But people do wake up and say, "It's going to be winter soon and we need to have a new roof on our house!" or "We need to renovate the basement so we have more room for our growing family." The feature or product the bank is selling is a home equity loan—and that's not very enticing. However, some benefits bank customers realize because of taking on a home equity loan are: new roofs, new swimming pools, new media rooms, new breakfast rooms, new game rooms, waterproofed or renovated basements, new garages, etc. Those are benefits customers value and want. In order to get them, they'll pay for the feature. They can envision the emotional, physical, and other benefits one or more of these loans will bring to their lives. As such, the sale of the home equity loan becomes much easier.

I've experienced the effectiveness of focusing on the benefits of what you're offering or bringing to an organization versus the individual skill sets you've acquired or features you're trying to sell.

Two years ago, my company conducted a survey of all of our past and current clients. We asked them to identify what they found to be most beneficial in working with me and my company. As a result of that, the following list came to life:

Top 10 Benefits our Clients have Realized Because of My Company's Consulting & Leadership Training:

We now:

1. Understand why and how to behave as managers and leaders instead of doers

2. Know how to clarify expectations of our teams

3. Have the skills and confidence to behave as leaders

4. Have a clarified future for our organization

5. Know how to build a stronger leadership team, employee population, and employee culture—i.e., build a stronger workforce

6. Know how to create simple systems and structure for our teams & organization

7. Have meetings that are focused and productive

8. Have fewer "difficult" situations because managers are better at managing "difficult" behaviors and conflicts promptly

9. Have more employees offering suggestions & solutions instead of just a select few

10. Have managers who provide constructive feedback and evaluate performance effectively

This list is now part of our standard marketing pieces and client proposals. Instead of encouraging prospective clients to buy three of our services: Strategic Planning, Succession Planning, or Leadership Training, we now share the list with them and say, "By working with us, you'll realize the following..."

In face-to-face meetings with prospects, their heads start to nod up and down as they read down the list. They want these things! They want these benefits! If my company can make that happen, they don't care what the specific services are, they just want those issues to go away!

As a result, our close rate has gone higher and we have little debate and pushback on our fees. Either they want the benefits or they don't. The choice is theirs.

Here's what I suggest you do instead: Don't view negotiations as negative. They're positive opportunities to advance your objectives, and possibly someone else's too. Being able to negotiate effectively is a key leadership skill and one that successful leaders intentionally hone. How else do they keep their organizations moving forward if they don't negotiate every now and then?

When negotiating for yourself, your position, or salary, negotiate just as hard as you do for your professional recommendations and positions. Get very clear on your professional value. Get very clear on the benefits other organizations have realized because of your efforts and skills. What have you helped others achieve because of your skill sets and capabilities? What problems did you help alleviate for others because of what you can do? What have you done? What have you accomplished no one thought possible or no one wanted to tackle? How consistent are you? What do your prior employers or clients say of you?

If you don't know, you need to find out. Simply saying, "I'm really good" isn't going to sell you to anyone. They want proof you'll make a positive impact in their world.

Let me also share a few pieces of advice on negotiating I shared in **Don't Let 'Em Treat You Like A Girl: A Woman's Guide to Leadership Success.** These ideas are focused on negotiating wages, but they are also key negotiating concepts to help with any professional negotiation situation.

Research what your position is worth in the marketplace.

Based upon your experience, skills, education, and accomplishments, what are you worth? You have to know what your realistic target compensation rate should be. Most people don't have a clue what that is. They just know what they'd like to earn. Compared to the true market rate, they may be high; they may be low. They're guessing. That's fine for them, not for you.

You don't want to overshoot, and you certainly don't want to sell yourself short. You've got to know what the right range is. Then if you like it—great. However, if you don't like the compensation rate because it's too low, you're prepared for a low offer and you won't mistakenly think you're being offered less because you're a woman. Instead, you'll know: that's the position's value.

You probably won't be able to find out exactly what others (i.e., women AND men) are making who have been in or who are presently in comparable jobs, but you can get a ballpark figure. Search the Internet for this data. Sites such as www.salary.com, www.monster.com, www.glassdoor.com, and www.womenforhire.com include tools and search features for this compensation information.

Also, contact your local chapter of the Society for Human Resource Management. Many chapters prepare an annual wage survey to gauge the wages in their respective areas. You may be able to buy one of the surveys from the local chapter. Go to www.SHRM.org to find your local chapter.

Once you identify what your salary range should be, realize that the prospective employer is not going to offer you the salary at the top end of the scale—unless you are THE expert in the industry. Most people aren't. So you have to be ready to anticipate that, at best, they're going to offer you something in the middle to lower end of the salary range. So now you have to determine what realistic salary you'd be content earning.

Identify your bare minimum package.

In a down economy, you may have to accept a lower minimum package than you'd otherwise prefer, if that means getting your foot in the door and a paycheck in the bank, it might be a wise move for you.

However, when the economy is more stable and opportunities are more prevalent, you have to identify what your bare minimum salary and package deal would be. That way, you're not quickly frustrated with your new position when the honeymoon period is over. What is the minimum salary you need to earn? Which benefits are a must, and which would just be nice to have? Which benefits do you actively utilize? Which ones are rather useless? You have to determine these tangible and intangible benefits yourself. This allows you to establish your "floor" for negotiating. Ideally, anything less than the "floor" offer constitutes a "No" from you, and you should confidently walk away.

Sample benefits include fully or partially paid medical insurance, 401(k) and other retirement plans, stock options, extra vacation days, day care, elder care, health or country club memberships, company cars, cell phones, hot spots and internet connections to allow you to work remotely, professional organization memberships, relocation costs, and position title enhancements.

Also, you'll need to determine which benefits would help position you for a future promotion or move. If the company can't offer you more money, seek a title change. That alone can carry a lot of credibility on your resume when you're seeking a promotion or have to look for work elsewhere: once a vice president, always a vice president. It doesn't matter if you were the vice president of a firm with only twenty-five employees, it was your title.

Identify your dream package.

Once you've identified your minimum salary and benefits package, identify what you'd love to receive: your dream deal. This exercise allows you to identify your "ceiling." Anything offered between your floor and ceiling is worthy of reviewing. Anything offered below the floor is a walk-away. Anything over the ceiling needs to be reviewed for any hidden catches. You can

"Whoo-hoo!" to yourself, but you need to control your emotions and identify the unspoken expectations of the employer (i.e., 75% travel, weekend shifts, relocation, etc.). The dream packages often hold them. You can celebrate after you've confirmed and accepted the requirements and the deal is sealed.

Negotiate the package.

Once you have identified your minimum and maximum (i.e., your floor and ceiling), you're ready to start the negotiation process. However, to do this effectively, you've got to be prepared. Do your homework. Talk to colleagues, search the Internet, talk to human resources professionals to get solid data on what's current and what's emerging in pay and benefits packages for your area and line of work. You want to look progressive—but realistic. Be clear in articulating not only the experience, skill sets, and capabilities you bring, but be very clear and articulate your accomplishments, and the benefits they can expect by having you join their team. Help them feel many of their problems melt away, if they can only get you to join their team.

Play Poker.

Compensation experts also suggest that you use your poker face during this process. Whatever nervous twitches or tendencies you have, be aware of them now so you don't default to them during the negotiation process. When you're nervous, do you raise your eyebrows or bite your lower lip? Do you bounce your knee or pick your fingernails? You want to convince those with whom you're negotiating that this process isn't a nerve-wracking experience for you, but rather a business deal to be approached logically. You will project a more professional image if you can negotiate your own compensation package from a non-emotional, professional perspective - so do your homework and internalize the skills, capabilities, and value you could bring to them.

Be Ready to Walk.

If you don't like what they're offering, be ready to walk—and do it professionally. If they don't meet your minimums, you'd better walk, or you won't be happy. If you believe you're getting backed into a corner and will have to start giving or caving in to hold onto your minimum (floor) deal, ask for something you know is a "giveaway" for them, (i.e., extra vacation, enhanced title, etc.) The objective here is to try to force them to give you something if you're going to have to give something yourself. This way, you win: you get your floor deal with something extra – and they win: they get you.

> *"All over the world when you test men and women for facial cue recognition, women test… better. It's a negotiation tool."*
>
> *— Michael Gurian, author and business consultant, founder of the Gurian Institute*

{ 10 } Stop Allowing Others to Tell You Who You Are

"What they call you is one thing. What you answer to is something else."

— Lucille Clifton, African-American poet

WHY: ALLOWING SOMEONE else to define you may well hold you back. People will have opinions about you, and—I'm sorry to say—not everyone will like you. Accept that and move on. If you're truly honest with yourself, admit to yourself you don't like interacting with every person you meet—that's normal.

However, don't think you're perfect or free of opportunities for growth and development. If you believe that, your entire life will be a challenge! Take feedback for what it is—feedback—and implement the helpful pieces. Forget the rest. Be true to yourself and be the best you, you can be.

I found one of my favorite pieces of inspiration inside a Chinese Fortune cookie: "The best thing you can do is get good at being you." I think that "fortune" speaks eloquently and concisely to the effectiveness of being true to yourself and what you want to accomplish in your career or life.

A leadership mindset is not stuck in the past or wound licking. It is intent on moving forward. You can't lead when you're looking backward.

As many of you know, for years clients knew me as: The Dragon Lady of Leadership Accountability. There's a story behind it, but suffice it to say, it was a good thing and my clients loved it and referred to "working with The Dragon Lady" with pride. The gist of being

The Dragon Lady of Leadership Accountability was that my clients (i.e., business owners and executive management teams) intentionally hired me to challenge them to be better leaders. They wanted me to help them identify (deleted words) ways they needed to improve as leaders. They also wanted me to hold them accountable to implement the needed changes.

Because of this, then and now, it's my job to be honest, fair, firm, and blunt with my clients. At the most senior levels, I've found my clients want the truth quickly and with no sugar-coating. It works for them. However, it doesn't work for everyone.

A few years ago, as I shared my nickname with several of my more successful clients. They said things such as, "That's why we like you. We know if we don't do what you tell us to do, we'll be in trouble!" Then they'd laugh. However, I also realized, they were the clients who were willing to make the difficult choices they had to make—at times letting go of select staff, ending product or service lines, or reorganizing their companies. They were willing to make the tough choices and take the difficult actions needed to move their organizations forward. So to them, working with The Dragon Lady was terribly helpful and a badge of honor!

In addition, I realized they were the type of people I most enjoyed supporting. My thinking, pacing, and style of communicating meshed well with theirs. I got energy from them and they gained insights from me.

However, I also learned my nickname didn't resonate with everyone. I lost a large six-figure contract because one vice president didn't like my nickname. I've had people tell me, "I don't much care for that dragon lady name or tone." And I'm fine with that. I honestly am, because I learned to quickly identify which words resonate and which don't to more quickly filter which new clients to accept. If in our initial conversation, a potential client is intimidated by my pacing, tone, or project outcome expectations, the client is probably not a good fit for me. I'll refer them to one of my colleagues.

Why? If they're intimidated or offended by my tone or pacing, my experience has shown, they're probably going to be resistant to making some of the hard decisions or taking the tough actions they may well need to take to move their organizations forward.

I don't need or want to make everyone happy. Not everyone will like my communication style, nickname or brand. What others say or think doesn't matter. It works for me and it works for my targeted and preferred clients—and they're who I want to work with to achieve success.

Here's what I suggest you do instead: Identify what it is you do well. What do your team members, colleagues, clients, customers, and others most appreciate about the work you do or the work you've done for them? What does your style of working with and helping others say about you? What they say about you is your brand. If yours is what you want it to be, take it on and leverage it. If it's not what you want it to be to enable you to work with and interact with the type of people you most enjoy, refine it.

Develop your network, skills, and work output that reflects what you want your brand to be. Don't try to please everyone or become what others want you to be. Don't let them label you or determine what your brand is or what success will look like for you. Define it for yourself and live it.

> *"Define success on your own terms, achieve it by your own rules, and build a life you're proud to live."*
>
> *— Anne Sweeney, President, Walt Disney Company*

Conclusion

IF YOU'RE A woman in a leadership role, congratulations! If you're a man in a leadership role, congratulations! I don't care. And I don't mean to sound snarky when I say that. What I do care about is that, as a leader, you focus on doing the job you're being paid to do. You bring all of your talents, skills, capabilities, and strengths to the role each and every day, knowing some days you're going to screw up big time.

On other days, you'll be exhausted because you were up the previous night holding your child's feverish head over a bucket. Life isn't always glamorous, it just is. But as a woman in leadership, stop doing things that are making your life harder than it needs to be. You don't need to be Wonder Woman. You just need to be the best you, you can be.

Continue Your Leadership Journey

Available at WBSLLC.com/Store

SOMETHING NEEDS TO CHANGE AROUND HERE
The Five Stages to Leveraging Your Leadership

- Are you tired of working 50, 60, 70 or more hours a week?
- Are you frustrated by what your team members don't do and can't figure out for themselves?
- Do you come in early and stay late just so you can get things done?
- Would you like to get your life back?

IF YOU ANSWERED YES TO EVEN ONE OF THESE QUESTIONS, YOU NEED THIS BOOK!

If you walk around complaining about your team or muttering to yourself, "Something needs to change around here," you're right. And it's probably you.

DON'T LET 'EM TREAT YOU LIKE A GIRL® — A WOMAN'S GUIDE TO LEADERSHIP SUCCESS

With insights gathered from women and men in leadership roles, Liz shares tips to help aspiring to experienced women leaders.

This quick-reading, insightful guide helps you identify:

- Which leadership traits are most admired
- What your leadership brand is saying about you
- How to manage conflicts and negotiations more effectively
- What "girly" behaviors you need to STOP!

This is a great resource for Women's Leadership programs!

Liz provides content-rich, interactive, skill-building presentations to groups large and small. Liz is known for her candor and her ability to customize her topics to meet your group's specific needs.

For more information, call +1(717)597.8890 or go to www.WBSLLC.com

About Liz Weber, CMC, CSP

In the words of one client, *"Liz Weber will help you see opportunities you never knew existed."*

Known for her candor, clear insights and straightforward approach, Liz Weber is a **sought-after management consultant, keynote speaker and seminar presenter**. She is one of fewer than 100 people in the U.S. to hold both the Certified Speaking Professional (CSP) and Certified Management Consultant (CMC) designations—the **highest earned designations in two different professions**.

As experts in strategic planning, succession planning and leadership development, Liz and her team are based near Harrisburg, Pennsylvania, and work with leaders to take their organizations:

- From no business strategy to enterprise-wide focus and clarity

- From no succession or workforce plan to enterprise-wide depth
- From a weak leadership team to a respected leadership team

Liz has supervised business activities in 129 countries and has consulted with organizations in over 20 countries. She has designed and facilitated conferences from Bangkok to Bonn and Tokyo to Tunis. Liz has taught for the Johns Hopkins University's Graduate School of Continuing Studies, as well as the Georgetown University's Senior Executive Leadership Program.

Liz is also the author of several leadership publications including:
- Something Needs to Change Around Here: The Five Stages to Leveraging Your Leadership
- Don't Let 'Em Treat You Like a Girl: A Woman's Guide to Leadership Success

- Stop So You Can Get The Results You Want

Liz's Manager's Corner column appears monthly in several trade publications, association newsletters, and internet resource centers for executives.

www.ingramcontent.com/pod-product-compliance
Lightning Source LLC
LaVergne TN
LVHW020932090426
835512LV00020B/3323